Truck Coloring
Book For Kids

I0772669

This Book Belongs To:

Please Give , Good Reviews The Book

ROCK CLIMBING

EXTREME
MONSTER TRUCK

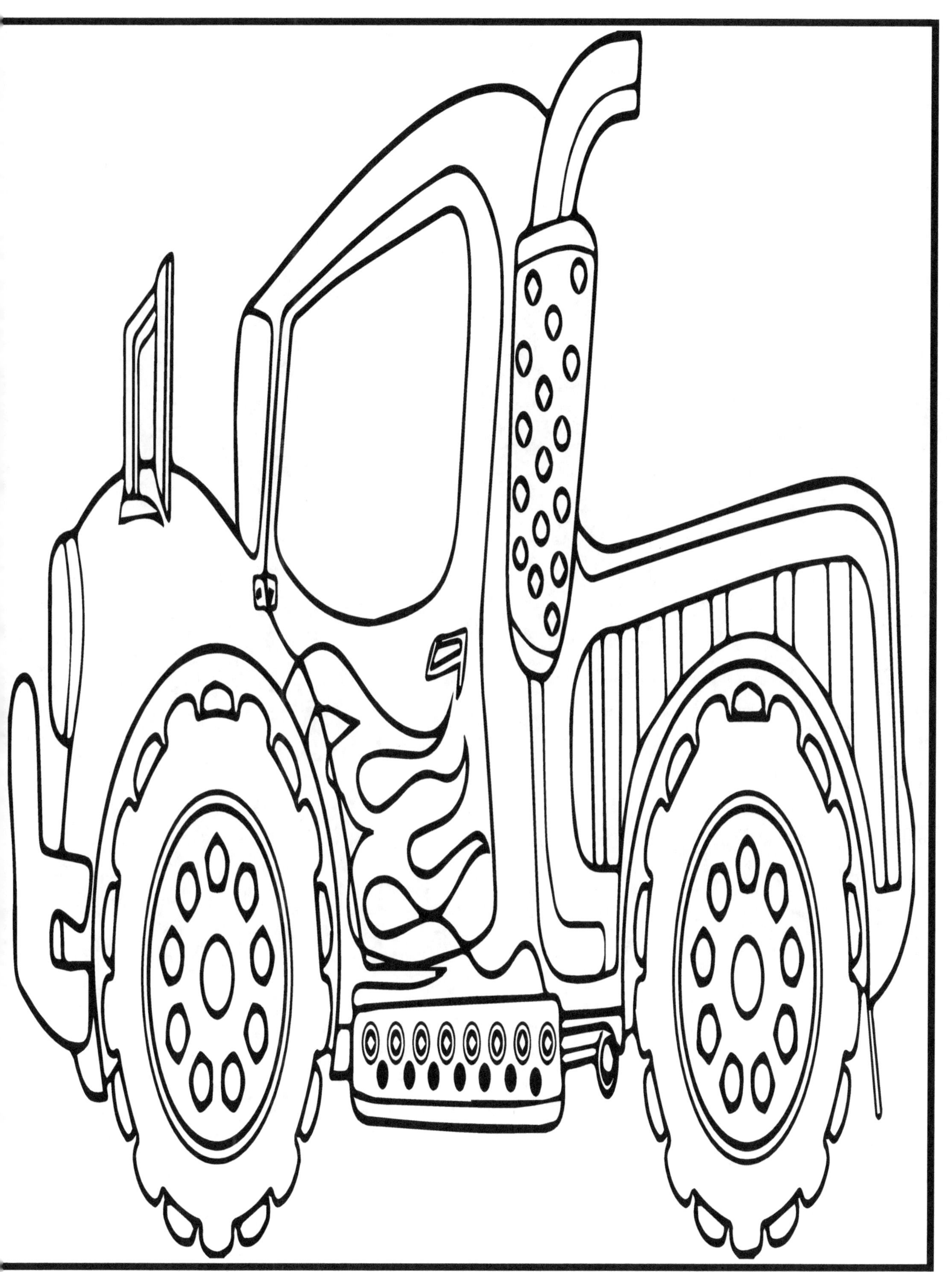

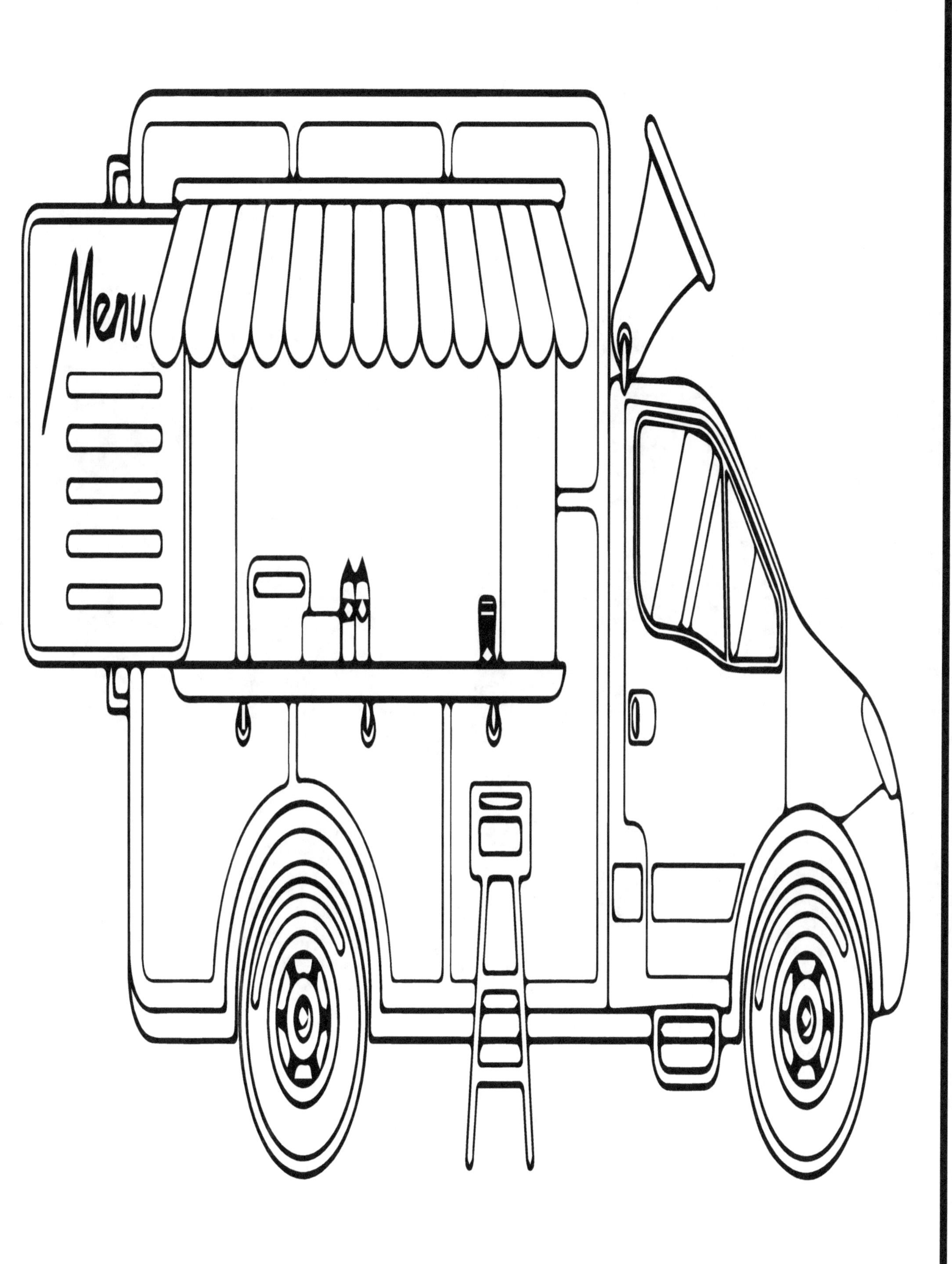
Menu

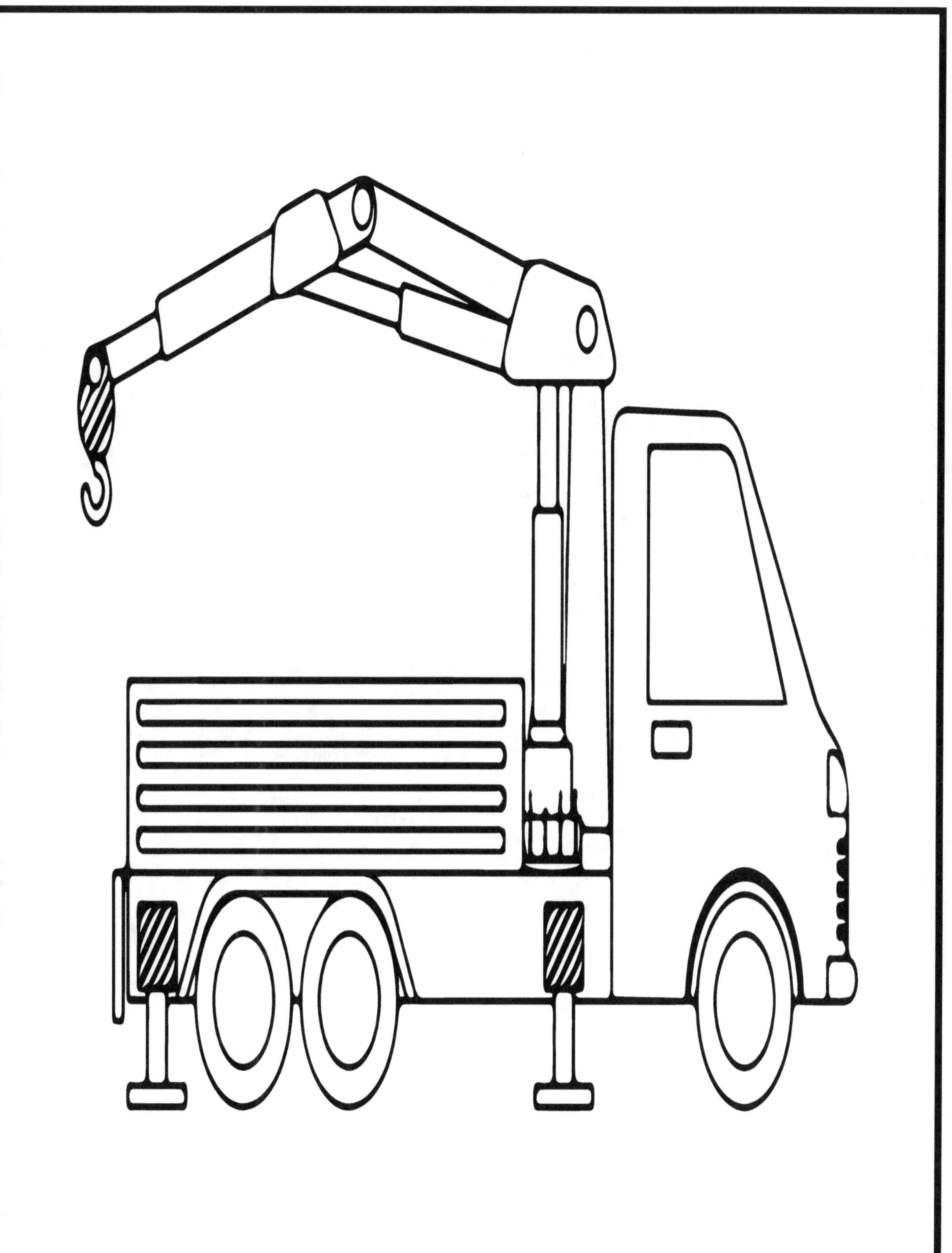

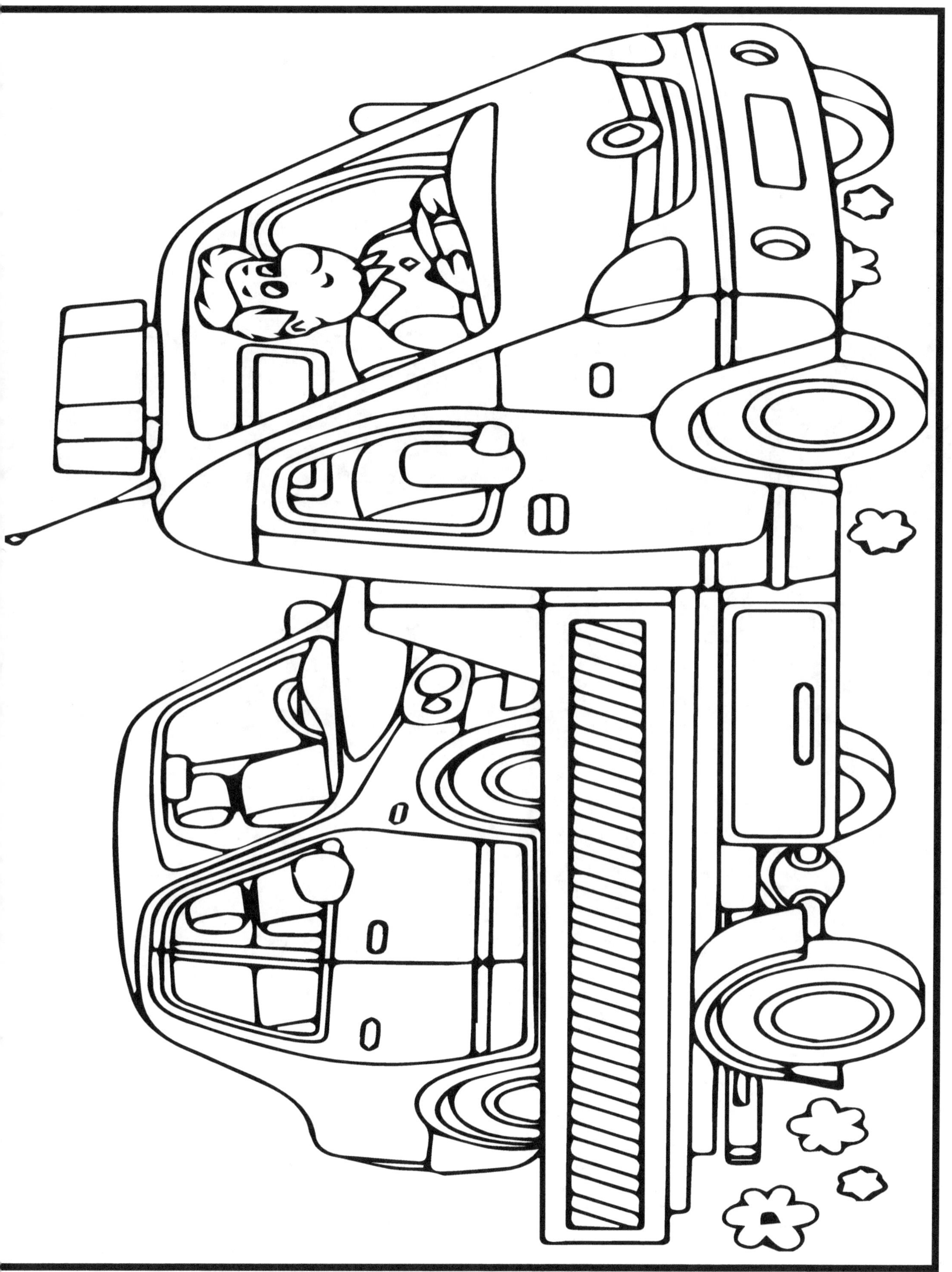

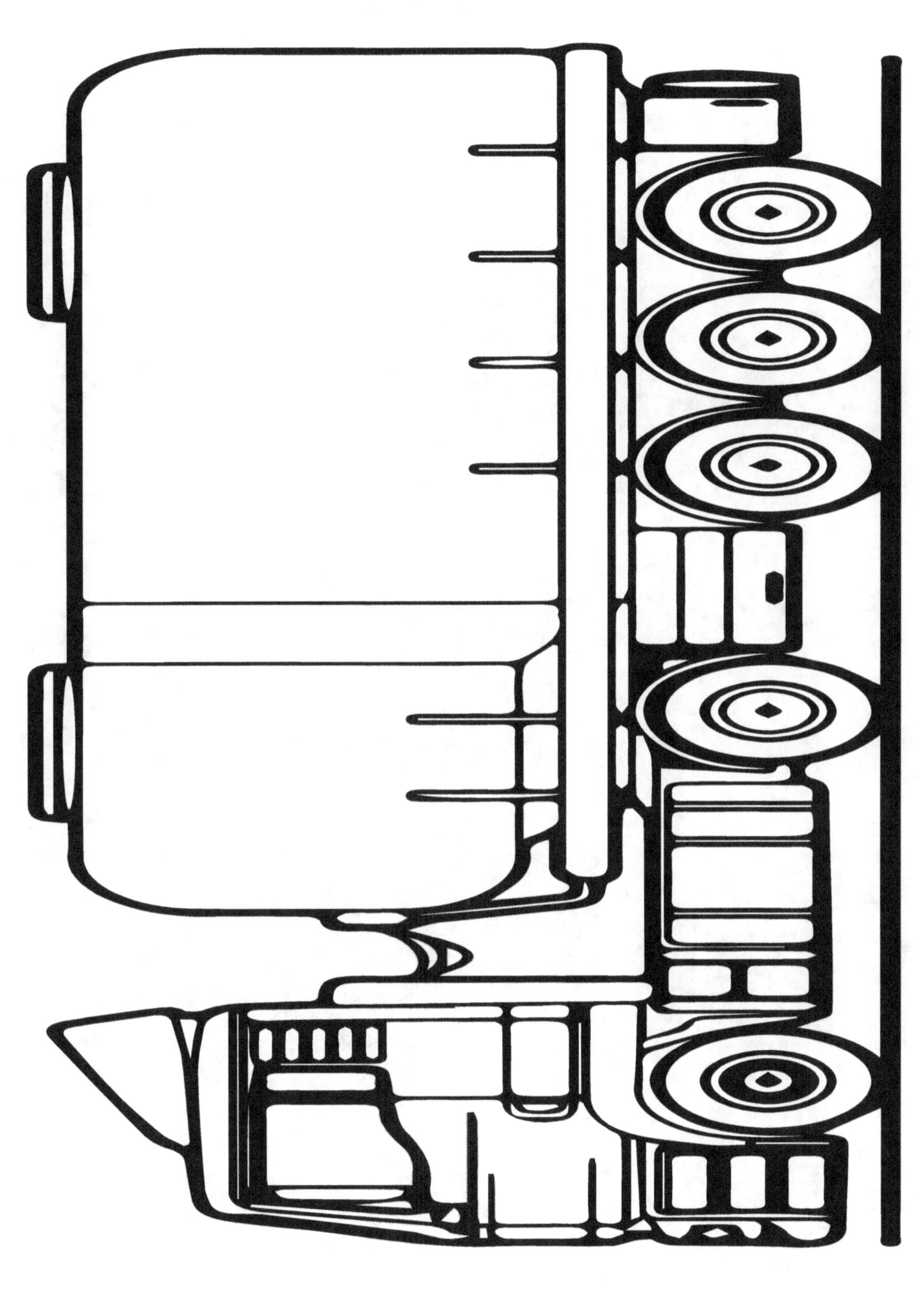